D1209666

LIBRARY SKILLS

A HANDBOOK FOR TEACHERS AND LIBRARIANS

by the California Association
of School Librarians

REVISED EDITION

Lear Siegler, Inc./Fearon Publishers
Belmont, California

ACKNOWLEDGMENT

The California Association of School Librarians expresses its appreciation to the 1958 Elementary Committee, Northern Section, of the then titled *School Library Association of California,* which pioneered in the field of library instruction by publishing *Library Skills.*

Walt Whitaker
CASL President
1971–1972

Jean E. Wichers
CASL President
1972–1973

ISBN-0-8224-4300-7

Library of Congress Catalog Card Number: 73-78275
Printed in the United States of America.

PREFACE TO THE REVISED EDITION

Even through the fun of games and devices, library skills are not learned unless they are used frequently. Learning, as teachers and librarians know, is more often retained when the objective of the learning experience serves an immediate functional purpose. With this goal in mind, each project included in the text indicates the behavioral objectives or skills involved.

Knowing how to use a library to complete lessons or to discover new horizons in books is a pleasant experience and a skill worth learning. Librarians and teachers will find that the projects and suggestions in this book offer a variety of ways in which library skills may be taught to encourage the regular use of the library at various grade levels. Most of these procedures may be adapted to the holdings of any library. The directions and preparations for each venture are simple and easy to apply. It is possible to develop these projects in either a classroom or a library situation, although the final proof of using library skills well is in the application of those skills in the library.

CASL STATE PUBLICATIONS COMMITTEE / 1972 1973

Bernice Gilardi
Dixie Elementary School
San Rafael

Mary Simons
Will Rogers Elementary School
Santa Monica

Martha C. Blalock, *Chairman*
Los Altos High School
Los Altos

CONTENTS

LIBRARY ORIENTATION

■ DRAW OUR LIBRARY (3-Up)

BEHAVIORAL OBJECTIVE: To be able to locate the different sections of the library.

MATERIALS NEEDED: Floor plan of the library. Lists as shown below. One copy of each for each child.

DIRECTIONS:

1. Give each special section of the library, indicated on the floor plan, a number.
2. Prepare a list of the areas represented, with a blank before each entry where children can add the appropriate number.

Example of a list:

______ fiction section
______ subject catalog
______ author-title catalog
______ periodicals (magazines)
______ reference (encyclopedias)
______ unabridged dictionary
______ transparencies
______ records
______ biography section
______ easy fiction (picture books)
______ nonfiction
______ sound filmstrips
______ circulation desk
______ 8mm loop
listening post
______ recorded books
______ game area
______ vertical file
______ student typewriter
______ map storage
______ study print storage
______ art print storage
______ filmstrip storage
______ 8mm loop storage
______ globe storage
______ recording area
______ darkroom
______ interest area

MYSTERY TITLES (4-Up)

BEHAVIORAL OBJECTIVE: To learn to use title and subject categories in the library card catalog.

DIRECTIONS:

1. The student selects or is assigned a special subject category. Working from the card catalog's subject and title cards, he prepares a list of ten book titles or stories that fit this category. He then scrambles the titles in the manner shown in the example that follows.
2. Other students are given copies of the scrambled list. They identify the titles and write them in normal form in the spaces provided. They are then given copies of the key so their lists can be self-corrected.
3. A file of the best, most popular lists and keys can be kept for duplication and use when needed.
4. All titles should be library holdings listed in the card catalog.
5. Students work *independently* in the school library.

MATERIALS NEEDED: Lists of scrambled titles. Keys, lists of titles in normal form. One of each for each student.

Example of a scrambled list:

SHREOS—NIFICOT — — — — — —

— — — — — — — —

1. tysim — — — — —
2. dilnas fo shreos — — — — — — — —

   — — — — — —
3. clakb loltians — — — — —

   — — — — — — —

4. enuddetharh — — — — — — — — — — —
5. gink fo het niwd — — — — — — — — —
   — — — —
6. het delgon ream — — — — — — — — —
   — — — —
7. blarmfads — — — — — — — — —
8. dolh het erin eref — — — — — — —
   — — — — — — — —
9. clakb etyabu — — — — — — — — — — —
10. ymosk — — — — —

Example of a key:

HORSES—FICTION

1. Misty
2. Island of Horses
3. Black Stallion
4. Thunderhead
5. King of the Wind
6. The Golden Mare
7. Flambards
8. Hold the Rein Free
9. Black Beauty
10. Smoky

■ MULTIMEDIA REPORTS (3-4)

BEHAVIORAL OBJECTIVE: To learn to use book and nonbook materials effectively.

DIRECTIONS:

1. Assign students a report on *any* subject of their choice.
2. Stipulate that at least *three kinds* of materials, including book and nonbook, must be used.
3. Limit length to two pages.
4. Require materials used be listed at end of report.

Example of an assignment:

Woodpeckers

a. nonfiction book b. filmstrip c. study print

■ HOW DO I FIND IT? (2-6)

BEHAVIORAL OBJECTIVES:

1. To be able to find books in high interest categories.
2. To diversify student reading.

MATERIALS NEEDED:

1. Book jackets
2. Railroad board
3. Laminating materials or rubber cement
4. File box
5. Subject dividers (optional)

DIRECTIONS:

1. Select book jackets of high eye and/or subject appeal.
2. Mount book jackets on sturdy backing. (If possible, laminate so they will not become soiled and worn too quickly.)
3. Print call numbers on reverse side of mounted book jackets.
4. Jackets may be arranged in categories such as "mystery" or "humor," or in alphabetical order by title or author in lower grades, in a browsing box centrally located in the classroom or library.
5. In upper grades, students may make selections and prepare them for the browsing box.
6. Upper-grade students may assist primary-grade teachers in this activity.
7. Browsing boxes must be updated frequently to maintain interest and effectiveness as instructional devices.

■ TEACH ONE TO TEACH ONE (K-6)

BEHAVIORAL OBJECTIVE: To become familiar with the proper use of equipment in the school library or classroom learning centers.

MATERIALS NEEDED: Equipment such as the following:

1. individual filmstrip viewer
2. sound-filmstrip viewers (either cassette or record models)
3. cassette tape recorders and playbacks
4. reel-to-reel tape recorders
5. blank tapes (both reel-to-reel and cassettes)
6. phonograph
7. overhead projector
8. opaque projector
9. 8mm loop projector
10. visual maker
11. slide projector

DIRECTIONS:

1. Select a piece of equipment that students need to know how to use independently for maximum effective use. (See the list above, under "Materials needed.")
2. Select a student who wants to use the equipment and is *willing to teach* someone else how to use it.
3. Arrange a time when the student can have sufficient practice in using the equipment under direct supervision.
4. When the student feels he knows the proper operation, have him tell or list the sequence of operating procedure.
5. Have him demonstrate the procedure to someone who has not been trained.
6. Remind all trained students to report and describe any malfunction of equipment as soon as they observe it.

■ LET'S PLAY LIBRARY (K-2)

BEHAVIORAL OBJECTIVE: To learn circulation procedures of book and nonbook materials in school library.

MATERIALS NEEDED:

1. Simulated library.
2. Check-out station.
3. Dater and stamp pad
4. Enlarged mock-up of library circulation card.
5. Books with cards in pockets.
6. Other materials that circulate to students such as filmstrips and viewers, records, cassettes and cassette tape players, recorded books, reel-to-reel tape players, study prints, and sound filmstrips.

DIRECTIONS:

1. Either librarian or student librarian assistants go to classroom at prearranged time with teacher.
2. Several sessions may be scheduled to include the following circulation procedures:
   a. Books
   b. Magazines
   c. Tape recorders
   d. Filmstrips
   e. Records
   f. Study prints
3. A large version of the card or the circulation slip used is shown and explained to the class. (If possible, this could be posted in the class prior to the training session.)
4. A mock library is set up with the librarian or student librarian behind the "check-out" desk.
5. Three or four students practice signing out materials.
6. These students each take a turn or two behind the desk with fellow students acting as patrons.

7. The lesson concludes with some "do's" and "don't" about the care and use of the type of material being demonstrated.

■ KNOW YOUR LIBRARY (4-6)

BEHAVIORAL OBJECTIVE: To become oriented to the library.

MATERIALS NEEDED:

1. 125 3×5" library cards in five different colors (25 each representing five areas in the library: 25 white, card catalog; 25 yellow, circulating books and periodicals; 25 green, general reference and nonbook materials; 25 blue, questions on library rules and procedures).
2. A labeled map of the library.

DIRECTIONS:

1. Number the color cards 1-25 in each group.
2. Make out three or four questions on each card and letter a, b, c, d (see the sample cards below). Caution students *not* to write on cards.
3. Give each student a map of the library. Direct the students to write the answers on the back of the map of the library, using the proper color number and labeling a, b, c, or d.
4. Two to four periods may be needed to complete the project.
5. Make out an answer key to speed check-up.

Sample cards:

Blue—No. 17—General Information

a. How long may fiction books be checked out?
b. How long may records be checked out?
c. What time does the library open and close?

d. What does an orange borrower's card in a book mean?

Yellow—No. 22—Circulating Books and Periodicals

a. Find a book called *The Mystery of Stonehenge*. The call number is 913.42. Is there an index in the book?
   Bra
b. Who are the characters pictured on the front of George Selden's fiction book, *The Cricket in Times Square?*
c. Find a fiction book by Armstrong Sperry with the word "courage" in the title. What color are the illustrations?
d. Find a copy of the *Audubon Magazine*. How often is it published?

Green—No. 9—General Reference and Nonbook Materials

Find Ref-700-G *Dictionary of the Arts*. Answer these questions:

a. In what work is "batten-and-button" used?
b. In what art is "dragging" used?
c. What Is a "pyx"?
d. "Woof" is used in what art?

Green—No. 14—General Reference and Nonbook Materials

In an encyclopedia, look at the article on Japan and find a colored chart comparing Japan and California in size and population. Answer these questions:

a. How much is the difference in size between Japan proper and California?
b. How many people are pictured in Japan compared with one in California?
c. List two cross references.
d. What is an important industry you would find in both Japan and in California?

White—No. 15—Card Catalog

Using the "P" tray of the author-title catalog answer the following questions:

a. How many books are there in this library by Leo Politi?
b. Who wrote a book called *Pecos Bill and Lightning?*
c. Who published *People Are Important?*
d. What is the call number of a book by Paul Brown called *Pony Farm?*

ALPHABETIZING

■ DICTIONARY PRACTICE (3-5)

BEHAVIORAL OBJECTIVE: To learn skill in alphabetizing words.

MATERIALS NEEDED: A list of words, headed by a pair of guide words, written on the chalkboard or distributed on worksheets.

Example of a list for seat work:

Here are two guide words and a list of twelve other words. Read these; then follow instructions below.

eastern to *neighbor*

helper	charming
partner	knotty
interest	friendly
meeting	laborer
journal	steamboat
grapefruit	brain

Instructions: If the list of words is put into alphabetical order, some of them will come before *eastern;* write "before" alongside these words. Some will come between *eastern* and *neighbor;* write "between" alongside these words. Some will come after *neighbor;* write "after" alongside such words.

DIRECTIONS: The sample list is prepared for seatwork and written individual answers. It may also be used as a class activity; assigned students reply orally and a student "clerk" or the teacher writes the answers on the chalkboard; in this plan, let the students also write the answers on their sheets for reinforcement.

Variation: This activity can be set up with lists on tagboard strips or on index cards, for individual use at a learning center.

■ ALPHABETIZING RELAY (2-4)

BEHAVIORAL OBJECTIVE: To learn speed in alphabetizing.

DIRECTIONS:

1. Mount some book jackets on tagboard.
2. Divide the class into teams of four to five students.
3. Give each team five to ten cards, face down, against the chalkboard.
4. On a "go" signal, the students alphabetize according to: author, illustrator, title, or as directed.
5. The winner is the team that beats "time" or is first to finish.

■ ALPHABETIZING (2-3)

BEHAVIORAL OBJECTIVE: To gain skill in alphabetizing.

MATERIALS NEEDED:

1. Pocket chart.
2. Word cards from publishers' reading series or cards prepared by the teacher. Select groups of words which give practice first in alphabetizing by initial letters, later by second and third letters. Also select words to teach "nothing before something."

DIRECTIONS: Students rearrange cards in a pocket chart in the correct order. Each child gets an opportunity during the three or four lessons. The children like the active participation.

Variation: Distribute the same word cards to students and have them arrange themselves in alphabetical order according to the cards.

■ AROUND THE WORLD (2-3)

BEHAVIORAL OBJECTIVE: To gain skill in alphabetizing.

MATERIALS NEEDED: Alphabet flash cards.

DIRECTIONS: One child stands beside an assigned chair. The teacher holds up a flash card and asks, "What letters come before and after this letter?" (This procedure is followed for the whole time the game is played. For lower levels more simple questions can be asked, for example, "What letter comes after this one?") The child who answers correctly moves on to stand by the next chair and so on until he misses. Another child then begins at the start. The one who travels farthest around the room, or the world, wins.

■ ALPHABET BINGO (2-3)

BEHAVIORAL OBJECTIVE: To gain speed in writing letters in alphabetical order.

MATERIALS NEEDED:

1. A graph card for each pupil to record progress in speed.
2. Worksheets such as those in the following example—with letters appearing in different order each time the lesson is used.

Examples of worksheets:

Part I

f—h	o—q	p—r	c—e	b—d	w—y
w—y	d—f	i—k	a—c	f—h	e—g
p—r	s—u	s—u	v—x	u—w	x—z
k—m	q—s	h—j	n—p	a—c	f—h
j—l	o—q	g—i			

Part II

—h—	—c—	—f—	—d—	—i—	—e—
—q—	—w—	—x—	—t—	—v—	—v—
—m—	—u—	—t—	—b—	—k—	—y—
—n—	—n—	—l—	—d—	—n—	—j—

DIRECTIONS: Work sheets are distributed face down. At a signal, the children fill in the spaces with letters coming alphabetically between the two given in Part I, and before and after the one given in Part II. The teacher writes the elapsed time on the board as pupils work, so that each may note the time he finishes. In successive lessons, each child may graph his progress in speed, with the teacher's help. Pupils may correct each others' papers to check accuracy. The teacher herself may check the papers as often as necessary.

■ USE OF THE DICTIONARY (2-6)

BEHAVIORAL OBJECTIVE: To use alphabetical order.

MATERIALS NEEDED: Dictionary for each child. Work sheets, in the example that follows.

DIRECTIONS: Prepare worksheets, as in this example. Be sure to use the words that are pictured in the dictionary the children are using.

Example of worksheets:

First: Put the following words in alphabetical order.

______________________	Weasel .... page ____
______________________	Peach moth .... Page ____
______________________	Knots .... page ____
______________________	Yak .... page ____
______________________	Flicker .... page ____
______________________	Fringed gentian page ____
______________________	Salmon .... page ____
______________________	Greyhound ..... page ____
______________________	Trees .... page ____
______________________	Solar spectrum .. page ____

Second: Find the page in your dictionary on which pictures of the things in this word list can be found. Write this page number in the "page" space.

■ SIMPLE ALPHABETICAL ORDER (2-4)

BEHAVIORAL OBJECTIVE: To recognize alphabetical sequence in words and call numbers.

MATERIALS NEEDED: Worksheets, as the example.

Example of worksheets:

1. Arrange the following list of words in alphabetical order. Some letters of the alphabet are missing.

black	______________	into	______________
ran	______________	no	______________
all	______________	eat	______________
did	______________	keep	______________
full	______________	open	______________

2. Arrange the call numbers on the make-believe books below as they should be arranged on the shelf of a library.

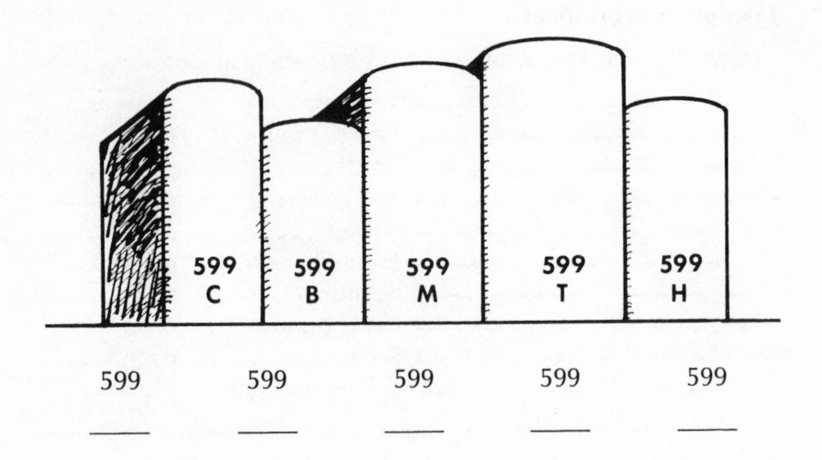

■ ALPHABETIZING PEOPLE (K-2)

BEHAVIORAL OBJECTIVE: To alphabetize last names.

DIRECTIONS: Have the children line up alphabetically by their last names when they are to be dismissed from the room.

■ ALPHABETIZE NAMES (4-7)

BEHAVIORAL OBJECTIVE: To arrange authors' names alphabetically.

MATERIALS NEEDED: Worksheets, ten names per sheet.

DIRECTIONS: The students alphabetize by last name.

Example 1 (2-5):

Robert McClung ________
Robert Lawson ________
Clarence W. Anderson ________
Lois Lenski ________
Ludwig Bemelmans ________
Marguerite Henry ________
Margaret Wise Brown ________
Walter Farley ________
Roald Dahl ________
Catherine Woolley ________

Example 2 (5-7):

K. M. Peyton ________
Julius Lester ________
Ann Petry ________
Elinor Parker ________
Rudyard Kipling ________
Rumer Godden ________
Cornelia Meigs ________
Carl Sandburg ________
Joseph Gollomb ________
Jeanette Eaton ________

Example 3 (4-7):

P. L. Travers ________
Janet McNeil ________
David Mackay ________
Selma Lagerlöf ________
George MacDonald ________
Kate Seredy ________
Andrew Long ________
Louise Rankin ________
Joseph Krumgold ________
Erich Kastner ________

Example 4 (4-7):

Edith Nesbit ____________________
Gerald D. McDonald ____________________
William Mayne ____________________
Louis Untermeyer ____________________
David McCord ____________________
Marchette Chute ____________________
Jules Verne ____________________
Arnold Adoff ____________________
James H. Dougherty ____________________
Laura Ingalls Wilder ____________________

■ ALPHABETIZE NAMES WITH TITLES (4-7)

BEHAVIORAL OBJECTIVE: To arrange author names in alphabetical order when book titles accompany the names.

MATERIALS NEEDED: Worksheets, ten items per sheet.

DIRECTIONS: Students write the names of these authors with the names of their books in the order of their arrangement on library shelves.

Example 1:

Cyrus Fisher, *The Avion My Uncle Flew*
Louisa May Alcott, *Little Women*
Esther Forbes, *Johnny Tremain*
Charlotte Bronte, *Jane Eyre*
Lloyd Alexander, *The Book of Three*
Elizabeth C. Spykman, *A Lemon and a Star*
Marjorie Kinnan Rawlings, *The Secret River*
C. S. Lewis, *The Lion, the Witch and the Wardrobe*
Anne Holm, *North to Freedom*
Lucretia P. Hale, *The Complete Peterkin Papers*

Example 2:

Eilis Dillon, *A Herd of Deer*
John Rowe Townsend, *The Intruder*
Arthur Ransome, *Swallows and Amazons*
Esther Wier, *The Loner*
J. R. R. Tolkien, *The Hobbit*
Daniel Defoe, *Robinson Crusoe*
Margot Benary-Isbert, *The Ark*
Mary Hays Weik, *The Jazz Man*
Robert Louis Stevenson, *Treasure Island*
Rosemary Sutcliff, *Warrior Scarlet*

■ USING GUIDE WORDS (3-6)

BEHAVIORAL OBJECTIVE: To apply alphabetical order.

MATERIALS NEEDED:
1. Three preschool type jigsaw puzzles.
2. Spray paint.

DIRECTIONS:
1. Choose puzzles that do not have identically shaped pieces. Spray over the picture until it is covered. Use the same color for all three puzzles. On the frame of each puzzle, print a pair of guide words from a page in a simple dictionary. The pages used for the three puzzles should be quite close together. Print on each piece of each puzzle a word that falls between the guide words on the frame of the same puzzle.
2. Scramble the pieces of the three puzzles, or of two of the three. One or two children work at putting the puzzles back together, using the guide words to determine which pieces will make up which puzzle.

■ COMPLEX ALPHABETICAL ORDER (2-6)

BEHAVIORAL OBJECTIVE: To alphabetize increasingly difficult words.

MATERIALS NEEDED: Worksheets, each with ten words to be alphabetized. Words are selected for graduated levels of difficulty.

Example 1:

I. 1st letter

band	all	full	no	keep
run	did	into	eat	open

II. 1st and 2nd letters

us	much	live	wash	never
you	ran	melt	this	these

III. 1st and 2nd letters

cans	cold	center	feel	fast
jump	drum	first	day	dirt

IV. 1st, 2nd, and 3rd letters

help	going	here	goes	have
gold	had	how	good	got

V. 1st, 2nd, and 3rd letters

every	sight	send	eve	send
sit	ever	sun	sung	even

Example 2:

I. 1st letter

us	________________	wash	________________
you	________________	these	________________
much	________________	see	________________
ran	________________	open	________________
live	________________	never	________________

II. 1st and 2nd letter

out	________________	draw	________________
cans	________________	just	________________

jump	______	first	______
do	______	give	______
every	______	have	______

III. 2nd letter

sort	______	snow	______
ship	______	slip	______
sun	______	self	______
sad	______	spin	______
strap	______	scar	______

IV. 3rd letter

gold	______	gobble	______
gown	______	got	______
goes	______	good	______
go	______	going	______
gore	______	gone	______

Variation: For a change of format, words may be on index cards or tagboard, each set of words in a different color or written with a different-colored felt pen.

■ TELEPHONE GAME—ALPHABETIZING (3-4)

BEHAVIORAL OBJECTIVE: To develop speed in alphabetizing.

MATERIALS NEEDED:
1. Sets of cards containing names and addresses.
2. Telephone directory.
3. Three players: operator, customer, and timer.

DIRECTIONS:
1. The customer asks for a telephone number, giving name and address. At this point, the timer starts timing the operator to see how long it takes to find the number in the directory.
2. After the customer has asked for three different telephone numbers from the same

card, then all change roles and the next person to become the customer gets a new set of cards.

3. After each player has had all three roles, the time scores are added to see who did the best.

Variation: Instead of using the published directory, make a directory for use in this activity. In large cities, the published directory may be too bulky, or its type may be too small for pupils in grades 3-4.

THE DEWEY DECIMAL CLASSIFICATION*

■ THE SYSTEM OF THE DEWEY DECIMAL CLASSIFICATON (5-7)

BEHAVIORAL OBJECTIVE: To learn the meanings of the divisions of the Dewey Decimal Classification.

MATERIALS NEEDED:

1. A chart showing the Dewey Decimal Classification. (A chart titled *How to Use the Library,* available from most library-supply houses, will serve.)
2. Ten large cards, readable across the room, each labeled with one of these Dewey Classification divisions and titles:

   000-099 General Works
   100-199 Philosophy
   200-299 Religion
   300-399 Social Sciences
   400-499 Languages
   500-599 Science
   600-699 Technology (Applied Science)
   700-799 Fine Arts
   800-899 Literature
   900-999 History

3. Small pieces of cardboard (players' cards), each with an identifying number on the back. The front should carry a sentence, a

*In the chapters on the Dewey Decimal Classification, Card Catalog, Parts of a Book, and Finding Information, many activities to develop skills are included. For background information to help the teacher or librarian prepare students for these activities, it is recommended that the Boyd, Santa, and Toser books listed in the bibliography be consulted.

definition, a phrase, or a subject relating to one of the Dewey Classification divisions.

4. Another set of cards (teacher's cards), smaller than the players' cards, with the identifying number large enough to be read across the room, and the corresponding sentence, definition, or the like on the back together with the corresponding Dewey division. If the teacher prefers, a list with identifying numbers can be used instead of this set of cards, and the teacher can call out the number instead of holding it up to be read.

Example of a players' card (front):

BOOKS ABOUT KNOWLEDGE OF
THE PHYSICAL WORLD

Example of a players' card (back):

4

Example of a teacher's card (front):

4

Example of a teacher's card (back):

BOOKS ABOUT KNOWLEDGE
OF THE PHYSICAL WORLD
500-599

Back of teacher's card only	Back of teacher's card and front of players' card
100-199	Books about the study of the truth or principles of all knowledge
200-299	Books about belief and worship of God or gods
300-399	Books about the study of man, his relations and institutions as a member of an organized community
500-599	Books about knowledge of the physical world
600-699	Books about skills and articles that help man
700-799	Books about skills and articles that give pleasure to man
900-999	Books about the records and studies of past events of all people
800-899	Books of the writings of a period or country
000-099	Books that have many of the other 9 Dewey Classifications in one book or in a series of books
030	An encyclopedia
423	A dictionary of the English language
912	An atlas
920	Lives of 10 people in one book
92 *or* B *or* 921	Life of one person in one book*
390	Conduct
290	Ancient mythology
328.1	Parliamentary law
353	United States government
595	Insects
598	Birds
620	Engineering
629	Airplanes

Note: This is a suggested list of card ideas only, and should not be used as the order of play.

*"B" is general elementary-school practice for biographies; it is not a Dewey classification. The number "92" is an accepted practice adapted from Dewey classification and indicates individual biography.

DIRECTIONS: Before the game begins, students should be told that Mr. Dewey divided all knowledge into ten separate classes (as the ten large cards and the Dewey chart show). Each of these ten major divisions may be further divided and subdivided appropriately, but in every case the books on one specific subject will have the same class number. Each book in a library is classified or given a class number before it is shelved so that all books on a given subject (such as stars) will be shelved together. Thus all the books about trees or rocks will be next to all other books about trees or rocks. Yet all these books about stars, trees, or rocks will start with the number 5 because they belong in the 500's, the science classification. Books about such legendary characters as Uncle Sam, Pecos Bill, or Roland receive a 300 classification because they tell about folklore personalities. However, books about Greek and Roman myths are classed in religion rather than folklore because the people of Greece and Rome worshipped such gods as Zeus, Juno, and Neptune. The *Dewey number* is the *class number*. Adding the author or Cutter number to this Dewey class number will give each book its own separate number for identification. *Library Skills* has no project for teaching the Cutter system.)

1. Distribute to the players all of the players' cards. Some players may have more than one.
2. Place the 10 large cards with the Dewey divisions and titles on tables or on a chalk tray.
3. The teacher holds up one small card, showing the identifying number to the players.
4. The player who has that identifying number on his player card takes his card to the place where the 10 large division cards are placed

and lays his card on the one that fits his card.

5. If he is correct, he leaves his card where he places it; but if he is incorrect, the teacher gives it back to him and puts the teacher's card into the pile to be used again.

■ SEQUENCE IN THE DEWEY DECIMAL CLASSIFICATION (4-5)

BEHAVIORAL OBJECTIVE: To learn the sequence of the Dewey Decimal Classification.

MATERIALS NEEDED: Copies of an exercise like the following, one for each student. The Dewey numbers are not on the student's exercise sheet.

Example of an exercise sheet:

A list of ten books is given below. On the short line at the left, write the Dewey Classification number for the book. Then, on the lines at the right, list the books in the order in which they should be placed on the shelves of the library. (You need not write the entire title; use the author's last name or the first few words of the title.)

574 __________	Hirsch, S. Carl. *The Living Community*	__________________
942 __________	Hutton, Clarke. *A Picture History of Britain*	__________________
398.2 __________	Sawyer, Ruth. *Picture Tales from Spain*	__________________
793.8 __________	Lemming, Joseph. *Fun with Magic*	__________________
599 __________	Zim, Herbert. *The Great Whales*	__________________
811 __________	Richards, Laura. *Tirra Lirra Rhymes*	__________________

398	Picard, Barbara Leonie. *German Hero-Sagas and Folk-Tales*	____________
634	Wall, Gertrude. *Gifts from the Grove*	____________
973.2	Fisher, Leonard E. *Cabinetmakers*	____________
636.1	Henry, Marguerite. *Album of Horses*	____________

■ CATEGORIES IN THE DEWEY DECIMAL CLASSIFICATION (2-4)

BEHAVIORAL OBJECTIVE: To learn categories of the Dewey Decimal system using pictures.

MATERIALS NEEDED:
1. Large heavy paper for charts.
2. Pictures.
3. Felt pens.
4. Sheets of colored paper.
5. Paste (glue).

DIRECTIONS: 1. Make a series of charts as follows:

Mount pictures on sheets of different colored paper to represent different categories of Dewey Decimal system, such as 500's, 600's, 200's, or whatever other category is of high interest to students.

2. Students draw or paste pictures on colored paper to represent covers of books. Label with Dewey Decimal number as it appears on the charts.

Variation: For older children the picture charts and book covers could be broken down into more specific divisions such as 520, Astronomy; 590, Zoology; 549, Mineralogy (rocks); 595.7, Butterflies; 598.1, Snakes.

■ REVIEW OF THE DEWEY DECIMAL CLASSIFICATION (3-5)

BEHAVIORAL OBJECTIVE: To group subjects into major Dewey classes.

MATERIALS NEEDED:

1. Bulletin board, flannel board, or Velcro display surface.
2. Cut-out numbers for several of the major Dewey classifications.
3. Pictures which can be posted under the numbers, representing aspects of the major subjects covered by the Dewey numbers.

DIRECTIONS: The pictures are distributed to the students. Each student, in turn, fastens his picture to the board under the appropriate Dewey number. This may be organized as a contest or may be used as a class activity without competition.

■ SHELF SEARCH (5-7)

BEHAVIORAL OBJECTIVE: To identify subjects from Dewey numbers on actual books in library collection.

MATERIALS NEEDED: Lists of Dewey numbers as in the example that follows. The space at the right is for the student to fill in with the subject of each number. These subjects, in parentheses, are furnished in the example but should not be given to the students.

Example of a list:

582.13 ______________________ (Wildflowers)
591.5 ______________________ (Ecology of animals)
793.8 ______________________ (Magic)
599 ______________________ (Mammals)
796 ______________________ (Outdoor sports and games)
970.1 ______________________ (Indians of North America)
916 ______________________ (Africa)
929 ______________________ (Flags)
398.2 ______________________ (Folk and fairy tales)
523.8 ______________________ (Stars)

DIRECTIONS:
1. The student is to find the books on the shelves with the Dewey numbers as listed above.
2. The student is to fill in the blanks with the subject of each number.

■ SHELVING PRACTICE (2-5)

BEHAVIORAL OBJECTIVE: To find the correct places for library books on the shelves.

MATERIALS NEEDED:
1. One or more library books for each child.
2. Strips of bright-colored paper, approximately 2″ × 9″, one for each book.

DIRECTIONS: Each child writes his name on the end of his strip of paper and places it in the book assigned to him, with his name and a few inches of paper showing. He shelves the book. After all have finished, the teacher checks for accuracy. The colored markers make it easy for her to find the books. Upper-grade children will be given more difficult books, with longer Dewey numbers, than will the beginners.

■ LOCATING FICTION BOOKS (2-3)

BEHAVIORAL OBJECTIVE: To use the author's last name to know where to find a fiction book.

MATERIALS NEEDED: Worksheets with lists of names, one for each student. The letters underscored in the following examples should *not* be underscored in the worksheets.

Example of a worksheet:

I

Natalie Babbitt
Clarence W. Anderson
Lillian Hoban
Leonard Kessler
Gertrude Chandler Warner

II

Virginia Lee Burton
Gene Zion
Carolyn Haywood
Beverly Cleary
Lois Lenski

III

Jacqueline Ayer
Evaline Ness
Robert Lawson
Eleanor Estes
Alvin Tresselt

IV

Sesyle Joslin
Leo Politi
A. A. Milne
Joel Chandler Harris
Jennie D. Lindquist

DIRECTIONS: The student is to underline the letter of the author's name that tells us where to look for a book by that author.

THE CARD CATALOG*

■ WHERE IS THE BOOK? (4-5)

BEHAVIORAL OBJECTIVES:
1. To develop speed in use of the card catalog.
2. To develop accuracy and skill in locating library materials.
3. To develop accuracy and skill in shelving books.

MATERIALS NEEDED:
1. 3″ × 5″ cards with titles of books which may be found in the school library.
2. Colored-paper markers.
3. Card catalog.

DIRECTIONS:
1. Distribute cards with book titles on them to class members. (Distribute titles throughout the alphabet to prevent overcrowding and to put all drawers of the catalog in use.)
2. Each child locates and takes to his place the book named on his card, using the catalog to find the call number.
3. When all books are located, each child exchanges books with his neighbor and replaces on the shelf the book his neighbor has originally located. For ease of checking, a colored marker should be slipped into the book. The marker could bear the name of the child finding the book *and* the name of the child shelving the book.

*In the chapters on the Dewey Decimal Classification, Card Catalog, Parts of a Book, and Finding Information, many activities to develop skills are included. For background information to help the teacher or librarian prepare students for these activities, it is recommended that the Boyd, Santa, and Toser books listed in the bibliography be consulted.

■ LOCATING TITLES IN THE CARD CATALOG (3-5)

BEHAVIORAL OBJECTIVE: To gain speed in the use of the card catalog.

MATERIALS NEEDED:
1. Book titles on small slips of paper.
2. Card catalog.

DIRECTIONS:
1. Each child is given a drawer from the catalog and an assigned place at a table.
2. A set of title slips to correspond with his card drawer is given each child.
3. The child places the slips in front of the catalog cards for the books. The librarian checks for accuracy.

Variation: The same activity can be used for author names.

■ CARD CATALOG PRACTICE (3-5)

BEHAVIORAL OBJECTIVE: To practice using the card catalog.

MATERIALS NEEDED:
1. Cards with questions, for appropriate drawers of the card catalog. Each card has one question. Sample questions are given, below.
2. Worksheets, 5 inches wide, for answers. These should have a space for the child's name and the question number. They also serve as marker slips (see the Directions).

Sample card questions:

1. Look under BIRDS and write down the names of two books you would like to read. Write down the call numbers. Find these books on the shelves.

2. Find this title card and write down all the bibliographic information: *Bits That Grow Big*.
3. Find this subject card:

   Sterne, Emma
   Mary McLeod Berthune. New York: Knopf, 1957.

   Call number 92
   B

4. Look under Brown, Margaret Wise and list four books by her and their call numbers.
5. Find a book about a famous war written by Bruce Bliven. What is the name of it and what is the call number? (*The American Revolution*. 973.3)
6. Who wrote a book called *Baby Farm Animals?* What is the call number? (Garth Williams, 636)
7. Find the title card for *By the Shores of Silver Lake* and then find who was the author. (Wilder, Laura Ingalls)
8. Find the subject card for BUTTERFLIES and then list two books we have and the call numbers.
9. Look at the title card for this book. Find the year it was published: *Wild Bill Hickok* by Garst, Doris Shannon. (1952)
10. Look under the guide card BEES and find a book called *A Bee Is Born*.

Note: The answers supplied for questions 5, 6, 7, and 9 should not appear on the student's question cards.

DIRECTIONS:

1. Assign three or four children to each catalog drawer. As they locate the card which will provide the answer to the questions on the cards distributed, they insert the question card in the correct place, with answer slip, for teacher checking.
2. Groups can be rotated, thus covering all material.
3. Cards pertaining to the separate drawers can be clipped together and kept at the rear of the respective drawers.

■ FIND US FAST (4-6)

BEHAVIORAL OBJECTIVES:
1. To practice locating a book by title, author, or subject.
2. To get information from catalog cards.

MATERIALS NEEDED:
1. Card catalog.
2. Worksheet forms.

Examples of worksheets:

YOUR NAME __________ GRADE ____ ROOM ____

(1) AUTHOR: Carr, Mary Jane

TITLE: __________

(2) AUTHOR: __________

TITLE: Covered Bridge

CALL NUMBER: __________

(3) CATS

AUTHOR: __________

TITLE: __________

PUBLISHER __________ COPYRIGHT DATE ____

YOUR NAME __________ GRADE ____ ROOM ____

(1) AUTHOR: __________

TITLE: __________

(2) AUTHOR: __________

TITLE: Familiar Quotations

CALL NUMBER: __________

(3) FISHES

AUTHOR: __________

TITLE: __________

PUBLISHER __________ COPYRIGHT DATE ____

Examples of worksheets *Continued:*

YOUR NAME ____________ GRADE ______ ROOM ____

(1) AUTHOR: Ness, Evaline ____________

TITLE: ____________

(2) AUTHOR: ____________

TITLE: Nine Days to Christmas

CALL NUMBER: ____________

(3) NEWSPAPERS

AUTHOR: ____________

TITLE: ____________

PUBLISHER ____________ COPYRIGHT DATE ____

YOUR NAME ____________ GRADE ______ ROOM ____

(1) AUTHOR: Wiese, Kurt

TITLE: ____________

(2) AUTHOR: ____________

TITLE: Wild Bill Hickok Tames the West

CALL NUMBER: ____________

(3) WHALES

AUTHOR ____________

TITLE: ____________

PUBLISHER ____________ COPYRIGHT DATE ____

Examples of worksheets *Continued:*

YOUR NAME________________ GRADE______ ROOM_____

(1) AUTHOR: James, Will

TITLE: ____________________

(2) AUTHOR: ____________________

TITLE: Johnny Tremain

CALL NUMBER: ________________

(3) JET PROPULSION

AUTHOR: ____________________

TITLE: ____________________

PUBLISHER ________________ COPYRIGHT DATE_____

YOUR NAME ________________ GRADE ______ ROOM_____

(1) AUTHOR: Duvoisin, Roger A.

TITLE: ____________________

(2) AUTHOR: ____________________

TITLE: Eddie and Gardenia

CALL NUMBER: ________________

(3) DOLLS

AUTHOR: ____________________

TITLE: ____________________

PUBLISHER ________________ COPYRIGHT DATE_____

DIRECTIONS:
1. Students are to fill in all information that is missing on the worksheet forms.
2. Students work in pairs, one pair to a drawer of the card catalog.
3. *Caution:* Be certain that worksheets given to students belong in the drawers to which they are assigned.

■ CATALOG CARDS (2-6)

BEHAVIORAL OBJECTIVE: To identify various catalog cards.

MATERIALS NEEDED:
1. Enlarged facsimiles of the various types of cards used in the card catalog. About three times actual size. (Some library supply houses sell facsimiles.)
2. Tagboard sheets for mounting the facsimiles, about 9×18″. Construction paper may be used but is far less durable.
3. *Or:* Transparencies of cards for use in the overhead projector if one is available.

DIRECTIONS: Use the cards to illustrate discussions and explanations of the parts of the cards and the ways in which they can be useful.

■ CARD CATALOG REVIEW (4-6)

BEHAVIORAL OBJECTIVE: To practice using the card catalog.

MATERIALS NEEDED:
1. The card catalog.
2. Work sheets with such questions and tasks as those in the samples that follow. Do not furnish the children with the answers supplied in the parentheses.

Sample questions and tasks for worksheets:

1. There are three kinds of cards in the card catalog. These are:
   a. ____________________ cards. They give the name of the person who wrote the book on the first line. (Author)
   b. ____________________ cards. They have the name *of the book* on the top line. (Title)
   c. ____________________ cards. They have what the book is about, on the top line, either in red type or in capital letters. (Subject)
2. The ____________________ in the *upper left-hand* corner of the catalog card gives us the location of the book on the library shelves. (call number)
3. The author card gives us at least four kinds of information. List all of them you can:
   a. ____________________ (complete name of author)
   b. ____________________ (title)
   c. ____________________ (publisher and place of publication)
   d. ____________________ (copyright date)
   e. ____________________ (call number)
   f. ____________________ (pages)
   g. ____________________ (illustrations)
   h. ____________________ (maps)
   i. ____________________ (index)
4. ____________________ cards are sometimes called "See" cards because they tell us to look for more information about a subject under another heading in the catalog. (cross-reference)
5. The ____________ drawers of the catalog would be the best place to look for *The Adventures of Tom Sawyer.* ("A')
6. Using the card catalog, find a book about BEARS and list the following information:
   a. Author ____________________
   b. Title ____________________
   c. Publisher ____________________
   d. Copyright date ____________________

7. Using the card catalog, find and list the titles of three books by Beverly Cleary.

   a. ________________________________
   b. ________________________________
   c. ________________________________

8. Using the card catalog, find and list *author* and *titles* of two books about "Miss Pickerell."

   a. Author ____________________________
   a. Title ____________________________
   b. Author ____________________________
   b. Title ____________________________

9. Using the subject guides in the card catalog, find *three* books about AUTOMOBILES and give the *author, title, and publisher.*

   a. Author ____________________________
   a. Title ____________________________
   a. Publisher ____________________________
   b. Author ____________________________
   b. Title ____________________________
   b. Publisher ____________________________
   c. Author ____________________________
   c. Title ____________________________
   c. Publisher ____________________________

DIRECTIONS: The students answer the questions by filling in the blanks.

THE PARTS OF A BOOK*

■ WHAT ARE THE PARTS OF A BOOK? (6-8)

BEHAVIORAL OBJECTIVE: To teach the student how to make the book work for him.

MATERIALS NEEDED: 1. At least as many *nonfiction* books as there are students in the class. Titles may include any of the following types:

Boyd, Malcolm. *Are you running with me, Jesus?*
Gilbreth, Frank. *Cheaper by the Dozen.*
Hamilton, Edith, *Mythology.*
Heyerdahl, Thor. *Aku-Aku.*
Heyerdahl, Thor. *Kon-Tiki.*
Information Please Almanac.
Kennedy, John F. *A Nation of Immigrants.*
King, Martin Luther. *I Have a Dream.*
Ley, Willy. *Watchers of the Skies.*
McWhirter, Norris. *Guinness Book of World Records.*
Maxwell, Gavin. *Ring of Bright Water.*
Momaday, N. Scott. *The Way to Rainy Mountain.*
Moody, Ralph. *Little Britches.*
Sone, Monica. *Nisei Daughter.*
Treviño, Elizabeth Borton de. *Where the Heart Is.*

*In the chapters on the Dewey Decimal Classification, Card Catalog, Parts of a Book, and Finding Information, many activities to develop skills are included. For background information to help the teacher or librarian prepare students for these activities, it is recommended that the Boyd, Santa, and Toser books listed in the bibliography be consulted.

Vanderbilt, Amy. *Complete Book of Etiquette.*
Vanderbilt, Amy. *Everyday Etiquette.*
Wong, Jade Snow. *Fifth Chinese Daughter.*
World Almanac and Book of Facts.

2. A question sheet for each student to complete.

Example of a question sheet:

1. Look at the title page of the book to answer these questions:
   a. What is the brief title of this book? Is there a subtitle? What, then, is the complete title?
   b. What is the name of the author as it is given on the title page?
   c. Who is the publisher of the book?
   d. Where was the book published?
   e. When was it published? Does the title page say?
   f. Who illustrated the book?
2. Where do you find the copyright date? (The copyright date usually is on the back of the title page.)
3. In some books there is a page that has a respectful statement, often worded "Dedicated to" someone, or just "To" someone; this page usually comes on the next leaf after the title page. The message is called a *dedication*. If there is a dedication in the book you are examining, who is named or described in it?
4. Is there an introduction, a preface, or a foreword in your book?
5. The table of contents is an outline of the entire book. Look at it to answer these questions:
   a. Where is the table of contents located?
   b. How many chapters are there in the book?
   c. Which chapter headings look interesting to you?
   d. Why is this part of the book important? (The table of contents gives an outline of the book and a brief description of what is in the book. It helps a reader to know whether he wants to read the entire book, or only a part of it, or even none of it.)
   e. How is the table of contents arranged? (The items in the

table of contents appear in the same order as the corresponding items in the text. Usually they have the same wording as the headings in the text.)

6. Is there a list of maps or illustrations for your book? Where does this appear?
7. On what page does the main part of the book begin? On what page does it end?
8. If your book contains a bibliography, an appendix, or a glossary, indicate on which page each begins. What is the purpose for each of these parts?
9. Is there an index in your book? If there is, how is it arranged? An index is a very important part of a book; it is not the same as the table of contents. In what ways are they different? (The items in an index are alphabetically arranged. An index usually lists many more items than are listed in the table of contents, and these direct a reader to the exact page where the item is discussed or presented. Hence indexes furnish a quick way to find information. In books that have no index, more time is needed to find an item of information. Some indexes are headed with special instructions on "how to use this index"; these often explain the system of indexing for maps or illustrations.)

Table of Contents	*Index*
General	Specific
Usually in front of book	Usually in back of book
Lists headings in order of appearance, with page number of heading	Lists items and names alphabetically, with page number where item occurs
Provides an outline of the arrangement or plan of what is in the book	Provides a guide to the various names and items in the book, but not to the plan
Requires knowledge of the subject, or complete reading, to find an item; may not enable a reader to find an item	Requires only knowledge of alphabetization and name of item to find it; enables a reader to find quickly any item that is in the index

Note: The information for appraising answers given after questions 2, 5d, 5e, and 9 should not appear on the student's question sheets.

■ THE ANATOMY OF A BOOK (6-8)

BEHAVIORAL OBJECTIVES:
1. To increase knowledge of the parts of the book.
2. To increase speed in using the book.

MATERIALS NEEDED:
1. Dictionary.
2. Worksheet.

DIRECTIONS: The student will use the dictionary to obtain definitions.

Example of questions for worksheet:

1. Define the following words:
   a. Dedication
   b. Frontispiece
   c. Foreword
   d. Preface
   e. Index
   f. Glossary
   g. Table of contents
   h. Appendix
   i. Bibliography
   j. End papers

2. At what location in a book will you find:
   a. Author's name
   b. Copyright date
   c. Place of publication
   d. Name of publisher
   e. Index
   f. Table of contents
   g. List of maps/illustrations
   h. Complete title
   i. Appendix
   j. Dedication

Answers:

1. The student's definitions should approximate these:
   a. *Dedication:* an expression of gratitude or respect which usually follows the title page and precedes the table of contents in a book.
   b. *Frontispiece:* an illustration facing the front page or title page of a book.
   c. *Foreword:* introductory remarks preceding the body of a book.
   d. *Preface:* introductory remarks preceding the body of a book. (*Foreword* and *preface* are used almost interchangeably.)

e. *Index:* an alphabetical arrangement by subject of the contents of a book.
f. *Glossary:* a list of technical or unusual words used in the book.
g. *Table of contents:* a summary or outline of the contents of a book, arranged as the information appears.
h. *Appendix:* supplementary or explanatory information, such as maps, charts, or bibliographies, which pertain to the book, but are not essential parts of the book.
i. *Bibliography:* a list of books which may have been used by the author in preparing his book, or which might be of interest to the reader who wishes to read more on the subject.
j. *End papers:* a folded sheet of paper which is glued to the inside of the book covers, front and back. Frequently the end papers are printed with maps, charts, or illustrations. (Many books, especially paperbacks, do not have end papers.)

2. Locations:
   a. Author's name: title page.
   b. Copyright date: reverse of title page.
   c. Place of publication: title page.
   d. Name of publisher: title page.
   e. Index: usually at the back of the book.
   f. Table of contents: usually at front of book.
   g. List of maps/illustrations: immediately after table of contents.
   h. Complete title: title page.
   i. Appendix: near the back of the book.
   j. Dedication: precedes the preface or introduction (some books do not have dedications).

■ WRITE YOUR OWN BOOK (5-Up)

BEHAVIORAL OBJECTIVES:
1. To use library resources in a creative project.
2. To have the creative experience of putting the parts of a book into proper arrangement.

MATERIALS NEEDED: Guide sheet for the student.

Example of a guide sheet

Select a place or a country in Africa that has people you find interesting. Your book will contain the following parts:

Title page: Title of your book, author of your book (your name), date finished.

Table of Contents: Chapter numbers, chapter names, page numbers. (Do you prepare this before or after you have written the book?)

Chapters: Four of them, as follows:

I. *The People:* Clothing; religion; food; how they earn a living. Do they grow crops or gather wild plants? Do they work in factories, or on farms, or do they herd cattle, or hunt wild animals, or catch fish? Draw pictures.

II. *The Places where People Live:* Are their houses like yours, or are they built of mud or stone or grass? Or do the people sleep in the open or in natural shelters? Do they have villages or towns or cities? What does it sound like in these places? Draw pictures.

III. *The Environment:* What is the climate like? Is there lots of rain, or little, or none? Are there big trees, dense forest, or desert? Is the environment the same as ours? How is it different? What does the place look like? Does the land have many hills? Mountains? Flat country? Are there lakes? Rivers? Ocean?

IV. *A Day in the Life of ——:* Pretend you are someone of your own age in that country, and describe a day in your life there. You *might* write this description as you would a diary: What did you do first in the morning? What did you have for breakfast? (Do you eat three meals a day, or more, or fewer?) Where did you go after breakfast? Was it to school? If so, describe the school, the teacher, the other students. Or did you go hunting or fishing, or do some sort of chores? Or did you go to work at a job? What is your work like? Tell what your family, your friends, your pets look like; how they sound; how they act. What do you do when you come home after you have been away during the day? What is the last thing you do before going to sleep?

Bibliography: The titles and authors of all the books or magazine articles you used when gathering information for this book. It should follow your last chapter.

Index: An aphabetical list of items in your book, with page numbers. It should include all personal and place names you mention, as well as topic items. It follows the bibliography.

FINDING INFORMATION*

■ USE OF THE DICTIONARY (7-8)

BEHAVIORAL OBJECTIVE: To learn special uses of the dictionary.

MATERIALS NEEDED:

1. One or more unabridged dictionaries, such as Funk & Wagnalls *New Standard Dictionary; Webster's New International Dictionary, Second Edition; Webster's Third New International Dictionary; Random House Dictionary of the English Language.* (The dictionary to be used should be checked to make sure it will furnish answers to questions asked of students. The various dictionaries do not agree in details.)
2. Worksheets for each student; an example follows. (The answers, in parentheses, should not be supplied to the students.)

Example of a worksheet:

1. What do the following abbreviations stand for?
   a. MFRS. (manufacturers)
   b. R.V. (Revised Version of the Bible)
   c. Ltd. (Limited)
   d. W.H.O. (World Health Organization)
   e. I.C.C. (Interstate Commerce Commission; International Control Commission)

*In the chapters on the Dewey Decimal Classification, Card Catalog, Parts of a Book, and Finding Information, many activities to develop skills are included. For background information to help the teacher or librarian prepare students for these activities, it is recommended that the Boyd, Santa, and Toser books listed in the bibliography be consulted.

f. R.C. (Red Cross; Roman Catholic; Reserve Corps)
g. C.J. (Chief Justice)
h. G.H.Q. (General Headquarters—*military*)
i. Q.B.P. (Queen's Bishop's Pawn)
j. H.R.H. (His *or* Her Royal Highness)
k. etc. (et cetera, *which means* and the like)
l. gloss. (glossary)
m. gm (gram)
n. T.V.A. (Tennessee Valley Authority)
o. w.c. (water closet; without charge)

2. Find the following proper names and give their meanings:
   a. John Bull (any Englishman; the English collectively; England)
   b. Roentgen, Wilhelm Conrad (German scientist, discoverer of Roentgen rays—X rays, winner of a Nobel prize)
   c. Maid of Orleans (Joan of Arc *or* Jeanne d'Arc)
   d. Neptune (god of the sea in Roman myth)
   e. Buffalo Bill (W. F. Cody)
   f. Lhasa (city, capital of Tibet)
   g. Dog Star (Sirius—the most brilliant star)
   h. Hamlet (prince of Denmark in Shakespeare's play)
   i. Maid Marian (Robin Hood's sweetheart)
   j. Nobel, Alfred (inventor of dynamite; founder of the Nobel prizes)

■ OH! MY WORD! (6-8)

BEHAVIORAL OBJECTIVE: To make, enjoy, and criticize word definitions.

MATERIALS NEEDED: Lists of words to be defined, with space for definitions; five words is a practical number. The words should include some that are difficult; one of them may be imaginary.

DIRECTIONS:
1. Five students are selected to be experts.
2. The experts (with teacher help if necessary)

choose a list of words to be defined and prepare worksheets with the list on them, providing space for writing definitions.

3. Worksheets are distributed to the class, and each student writes his definition of each word.
4. Each student reads his definition. The class and teacher decide which definition or definitions are correct.
5. After all definitions have been read, the correct definitions are read again and the students correct their papers.
6. Five new experts are chosen to select the next list of words and prepare the worksheets. For the best results, encourage the students to work in teams, helping each other to think up both correct definitions and definitions that are plausible and humorous. Let the teams work in the library.

Sample word with imaginary definitions:

FLOURMETER
—a meter used to measure flowers
—a meter or screen used to measure the color of X rays
—a meter or screen used to measure the purity of water
—a meter to measure percent of corn and wheat flour in a pancake mix
—a meter to measure the quantity of caraway seeds in rye bread

■ FINDING GENERAL INFORMATION (6-8)

BEHAVIORAL OBJECTIVE: To gain ability in selecting correct sources for finding information.

MATERIALS NEEDED: 1. Copies of Jessie Boyd's *Books, Libraries, and You.*

2. Encyclopedias such as *World Book, Compton's, Colliers.*
3. Other reference books, such as *Who's Who in America, Twentieth Century Authors, Junior Book of Authors, Current Biography.*
4. Worksheets. Answer keys, based on the reference books available in the library.

Example of a worksheet:

Answer the following questions and give the source of each of your answers by naming the book's title, the volume, and the page number. If you already know the answer without looking it up, give the source where your answer can be checked.

1. What are the titles for three (3) songs composed by Irving Berlin?
2. What are the names of two pictures painted by Vincent van Gogh?
3. Whom did Herbert Hoover marry?
4. Name four books written by Samuel Clemens.
5. What offices did Franklin D. Roosevelt hold before becoming President?
6. Of what college was Woodrow Wilson President?
7. What was the birthdate of the late President Eisenhower?
8. For what was Clara Barton famous?
9. What is the copyright date of the most recent encyclopedia in the library?
10. Where was Susan B. Anthony born?

DIRECTIONS:

1. Have the students read Boyd's *Books, Libraries, and You,* Chapter 8, "Encyclopedias," pp. 103-121, and Chapter 9, "Other Reference Books," pp. 103-121. These will help students to understand the special features of each encyclopedia and basic reference book.
2. Distribute worksheets and let the students prepare their answers. Then distribute answer keys and let them self-correct their work.

■ ENCYCLOPEDIA ROUND-UP (6-8)

BEHAVIORAL OBJECTIVE: To learn the use of encyclopedias as first sources of information.

MATERIALS NEEDED:
1. Any encyclopedia.
2. Worksheets. Answer keys, based on the encyclopedia the students will use.

Example of a worksheet:

Write out answers to the following questions. Give the source where you obtained the information (title, volume number, pages). Tell how you located the information: A—by using the main alphabetical arrangement. B—by using the index. C—by using the cross references. (You may have used any one or all three of these.)

1. In what part of the United States did the following Indian tribes live: Cherokee, Miwok, Sioux, Pueblo, Seminole, Iroquois, and Klikitat?
2. For what is ambergris used? Is it a valuable substance?
3. For what is Edward Jenner famous? How did he happen to make this great discovery?
4. What was Paul Revere's occupation?
5. Who organized the Green Mountain boys? In what war did they fight?
6. What was the nickname of Thomas J. Jackson? Why was he so named?
7. What are the qualifications for admission to West Point?
8. Who painted "Mona Lisa"? What are two other paintings by the same artist?
9. Who was the real Robinson Crusoe?
10. Where are most flies born?
11. How do crickets sing?
12. How long can a hippopotamus stay under water?

DIRECTIONS:
1. Explain the project to the students and distribute the worksheets.

2. Distribute the answer keys and let the students self-correct their answers.

■ HOW TO LOOK UP INFORMATION ABOUT REAL PEOPLE (5-8)

PROJECT OBJECTIVE: To give a general set of suggestions for finding biographical information.

MATERIALS NEEDED: An information sheet to be given to each student.

Example of an information sheet:

1. Check the card catalog to see what biographies we have in our library. Look for the last name first.
2. Encyclopedias will give some information about most famous people. Use the encyclopedia index to lead you quickly to biographical information.
3. Some unabridged dictionaries give brief data on VERY famous people.
4. If the person is an author of junior high stories or reference books, look in *Junior Authors*. If there is a pamphlet box on the shelves which has information about authors of the books, consult that for further information.
5. To "get to know" a person find out about his interests, his activities, his professional works. Find out if the time when he lived influenced his career.
6. If the person in whom you are interested is still alive, you may find out something about him in the *Information Please Almanac*, the *World Almanac, Who's Who, Who's Who in America*, or in a regional government publication like the *California Blue Book*. Consult these.
7. *The Readers' Guide to Periodical Literature* is an excellent way to find the latest information on currently important people. Even people from earlier times, like Shakespeare, are often discussed in current magazines.

■ GETTING TO KNOW THEM (6-8)

BEHAVIORAL OBJECTIVE: To learn to locate biographical information.

MATERIALS NEEDED:

1. Any of the following: *New Century Cyclopedia of Names, Contemporary Authors, Twentieth Century Authors, First Supplement to Twentieth Century Authors, Junior Book of Authors, Readers' Guide to Periodical Literature, Who's Who, Who's Who in America,* general Encyclopedias, unabridged Dictionaries, *Negro Almanac, Webster's Biographical Dictionary, Current Biography,* the card catalog.
2. List of names for biographical research.

Sample list:

[List of the sources available in your school]

Use the above sources to locate biographical information on any five of the following real people. On a 3×5″ card write your name, the person's name, his or her occupation or profession and place of birth, and the source of your information.

1. Aristotle
2. Thomas Jefferson
3. Jackie Robinson
4. Ralph Moody
5. Charles Lindbergh
6. Richard M. Nixon
7. Thor Heyerdahl
8. Isaac Asimov
9. P. T. Barnum
10. Ann Landers
11. Sandy Duncan
12. Bret Harte
13. William Shakespeare
14. Plato
15. Joy Adamson
16. Leonard Bernstein
17. Louis Pasteur
18. James Baldwin
19. Orson Welles
20. Pablo Picasso
21. Flip Wilson
22. Juan Marichal
23. Diahann Carroll
24. Florence Nightingale
25. Pearl Buck
26. Carry Nation

■ THE GREAT SEARCH (7-8)

BEHAVIORAL OBJECTIVE: To have additional opportunities to use reference skills.

MATERIALS NEEDED: Sheets containing search questions.

Sample questions:

Answer each question and give the exact source (title, page, edition of book used) in which you find the answer.

1. André Gide is a French author. On what page of what reference book can you find information about him?
2. Felix Salten, who is the author of *Bambi,* can be found on what page of *Junior Book of Authors*?
3. In what reference book and on what page can you find information on Louisa May Alcott, author of *Little Women*?
4. There is an article on Nordhoff and Hall in the *Junior Book of Authors.* What book did they write that you may have read?
5. Where can a person find information on the French horn?
6. Leontyne Price is an opera singer. Where can you find information about her?
7. Leonard Bernstein is a famous symphony conductor. Where can you find information about him?
8. Where can you find an article about Charles Dickens?
9. On what page of what reference book is there an article on Walter Farley?
10. Where do you find an article on the baseball star, Willie Mays?
11. Are the following people listed in *Webster's Biographical Dictionary:* José Iturbi, Marc Chagall, Winston Churchill?
12. On what river is Fairbanks, Alaska?
13. Where do you find an article on Mark Twain?
14. Where is information on the recorder?
15. What lake is on the east side of the Grand Tetons?

16. In what volume of *Current Biography* would you find information on Chou En-lai?
17. What large town is situated within 15 miles of North Pole, Alaska?
18. Find an article on Grandma Moses and list your source.
19. From what material is nylon made?
20. Where is an article on Glen Campbell?

■ REFERENCE RACE (6-8)

BEHAVIORAL OBJECTIVE: To form the practice of applying reference skills independently.

MATERIALS NEEDED:

1. Encyclopedias, atlases, almanacs, dictionaries, quotation books, and other basic biographical and reference sources.
2. A set of 100 reference questions (numbered), typed on separate cards, one to a card. Twenty sample questions are given below.
3. A list of the class members with two or more blanks after each name.

Sample questions:

1. Find an address for José Ferrer. (*Who's Who in America; Who's Who*)
2. Locate a map of Burgoyne's invasion, 1777. (*Historical Atlas; Atlas of American History*)
3. Was George Sand a man or a woman? Give the correct name. (*Webster's Biographical Dictionary*; *New Century Cyclopedia of Names*)
4. Who was the vice president for George Washington? (*World Almanac; Information Please Almanac*)
5. What is the net paid circulation for the *San Francisco Chronicle* (for a specific year)? (*Information Please Almanac*)

6. What is Nancy Hanks' occupation? (*Current Biography*)
7. What is the national anthem of Turkey, and when was it adopted? (*Americana Encyclopedia*)
8. Find a map showing the surface transport facilities of the world. (*Goode World Atlas; Rand McNally World Atlas*)
9. What city has the greatest number of telephones? How many? (*Compton's; World Almanac; Information Please Almanac*)
10. What is a good source of Vitamin A? (*World Book; Information Please Almanac*)
11. Find current information on the Common Market in Western Europe. (*Readers' Guide to Periodical Literature*)
12. Find a current reference to *Romeo and Juliet*. (*Readers' Guide to Periodical Literature*)
13. What does number-nip mean? (*Funk & Wagnalls New Standard Dictionary*, unabridged)
14. From what source did the following quotation come? "Some are born great, some achieve greatness, and some have greatness thrust upon 'em." (*Bartlett's Familiar Quotations; Home Book of Quotations; New Cyclopedia of Practical Quotations*)
15. Who offered the sage advice, "In baiting a mouse-trap with cheese, always leave room for the mouse"? (*Bartlett's Familiar Quotations*)
16. "It is not good a sleeping hound to wake." Who wrote it and in what literary masterpiece? (*New Cyclopedia of Practical Quotations*)
17. Find the author and title for the following selection: "None of them knew the color of the sky." (*Bartlett's Familiar Quotations*)
18. What is Fig Sunday? (*Funk and Wagnalls New Standard Dictionary*, unabridged); *Webster's New International Dictionary*, second edition, unabridged)
19. "We beat them today or Molly Stark's a widow." Who said it and on what occasion? (*Bartlett's Familiar Quotations*)
20. Who used the pseudonym Runnymede? (*New Century Cyclopedia of Names*)

Note: The answers in parentheses are not given to the student.

DIRECTIONS: Issue cards at random to individual students; let them bring and show you acceptable answers. Write the number of the correctly answered question after the student's name and issue him another card. Continue as long as time and interest permit.

■ IF IT'S NEW . . . (6-8)

BEHAVIORAL OBJECTIVE: To learn how to find the most recent information.

MATERIALS NEEDED:
1. *Readers' Guide to Periodical Literature* or *The Abridged Readers' Guide to Periodical Literature,* and *How to Use the Readers' Guide* (copies of these pamphlets are available from the publisher without charge).
2. Question sheets.

Example of a question sheet:

Use [either edition of] *Readers' Guide* to locate (in the front) the page with the explanation of how to "decipher" the sample entry. Also find the page with the abbreviations for the titles of the magazines indexed. Remember *Readers' Guide* is an alphabetical index to periodicals (magazines) but it only directs by author and subject. Remember, too, magazines are published at frequent intervals (periodically) so they can give the very latest information on many subjects. Answer these questions:

1. Which magazines indexed in *Readers' Guide* may be found in your library? List them.
2. Write the name of your favorite movie star, baseball player, and author on separate cards. Look in *Readers' Guide* to see if these names are listed (you may need to look in more than one issue to find the name). How many references (citations) do you find for each?

3. Find a review of a currently popular moving picture. How did you locate it?

■ COMPARISON OF REFERENCE RESOURCES (6-8)

BEHAVIORAL OBJECTIVE: To learn selectivity in the use of reference materials.

MATERIALS NEEDED:
1. Reference books.
2. Work sheets with instructions for the student.

Example of instructions for the student:

You are to compare several reference sources and make a report of how they are organized. You are also to select a topic and compare how these reference sources deal with it. Some possible kinds of topics:

Black History	The Olympic Games
Mexican-American Culture	Indian Culture
Taiwan	Red China
Drugs	Alcoholic Beverages
Ecology	

These are very broad subjects. You may want to select a more specific topic for your comparison; choose one for which the reference resources offer information. Try as many of the reference resources as you can; some may have nothing on your topic.

In the column of your worksheets headed "N.V." list the number of volumes in the resource.

In the column headed "Index," indicate where the index is located in the resource. You may use these abbreviations: *sep.* = in separate volume; *each* = in each volume, at the end; *last* = in the last volume; *none* = no index.

In the column headed "Use of Pictures," indicate *many, some,* or *none.*

In the group of columns headed "Research Topic," indicate the volume and page where the information on your topic is located (it may be at more than one place); indicate the amount of information given as so many lines or so many columns; indicate the number of pictures (none if none).

A sample list of reference sources:

Funk and Wagnalls New Standard Dictionary of the English Language, unabridged.
Webster's Third New International Dictionary, unabridged.
Cassell's Spanish Dictionary.
Webster's Biographical Dictionary.
Webster's Geographical Dictionary.
Britannica Junior Encyclopedia.
Collier's Encyclopedia.
Compton's Encyclopedia and Fact Index.
Encyclopedia Americana.
Encyclopedia International.
Merit Student Encyclopedia.
Our Wonderful World.
The World Book.
Columbia Encyclopedia.
The Lincoln Library of Essential Information.
The American Negro Reference Book.
New Book of Knowledge.
New Century Cyclopedia of Names.
McGraw-Hill Encyclopedia of Science and Technology.
Goode's World Atlas.
Life Pictorial Atlas of the World.
Rand McNally Cosmopolitan World Atlas.
Lands and Peoples.

If other resources are available in your library, they should be included. It is useful to number them in the worksheets. Avoid listing resources not available to your students.

Example of a worksheet:

COMPARISON OF REFERENCE RESOURCES

NAME: ______________________ DATE: ______________

TOPIC: ______________________

Reference Resources	N.V.	Index	Use of Pictures	Research Topic			
				Location		Amount	Pictures
				Vol.	pp.		
1. Funk & Wagnalls New Standard Dictionary of the English Language, unabridged							
2. Webster's Third New International Dictionary, unabridged							
3. Cassell's Spanish Dictionary							
4. Webster's Biographical Dictionary							
5. Webster's Geographical Dictionary							

APPRECIATION

■ BOOK TRAIN (K-3)

BEHAVIORAL OBJECTIVE: To stimulate student interest in reading more books.

MATERIALS NEEDED:
1. All colors of construction paper.
2. Rug yarn.
3. Long, narrow bulletin board.

DIRECTIONS: The teacher makes an attractive train out of colored construction paper with a little flat car for each child in the class. (Black rug yarn makes an effective track.) The students read books as they choose.

a. For each book read, the student adds a colored symbol to his car's load. A good symbol is a "book" cut from construction paper.

b. Teachers may require an oral report or a brief written report as a prerequisite for adding to the load.

c. Names of authors, titles, and dates of completed reading may add variety to the student's load.

■ WHAT'S THE NAME OF MY STORY? (3-5)

BEHAVIORAL OBJECTIVES:
1. To be able to select important ideas.
2. To be able to retell a story orally.

3. To stimulate student interest in more accurate reading.

MATERIALS NEEDED:
1. Library books.
2. Drawing paper.
3. Bulletin board.

DIRECTIONS:
1. The student is expected to read a library book and prepare to present it to the class on Friday afternoon. He will tell orally about the story of his book, display a picture or pictures on the bulletin board to illustrate it, and put a scrambled title* on the bulletin board. He will not reveal the actual title to the class until after his Friday presentation. As he reads his book, he will plan:
   a. His *illustration* of the story, based on the main points.
   b. *How much* of the story he will tell orally.
   c. The *manner* in which he will tell the story. His object is to make other students *want* to guess the story title.
   d. The scrambled title for his story.
2. Pictures and scrambled titles are put on the "What's the Name of My Story?" bulletin board during the week and remain until the Friday afternoon presentation time.
3. A student starts by telling about the story which he has illustrated. Other students attempt to identify his story and unscramble the title to name the story.
4. The student who first guesses the correct title or comes nearest to guessing it takes the next turn.

*Scrambled titles: These can be done by having the words scattered over the bulletin board, as "Huckleberry" in one corner and "Finn" in another place. A more difficult method may be scrambled syllables, as *"Finn/ber/Huck/le/ry"*; most difficult, letters juxtaposed, as *"Nifn Rrykchuelbe."*

■ BOOK FAIR (K-8)

BEHAVIORAL OBJECTIVES:

1. To observe Brotherhood Week and Black History Week.
2. To make students aware of the various ethnic literatures.
3. To make ethnic literary material available to students and the community, by displaying and selling books.

PEOPLE NEEDED:

1. A book-selection committee: parents, librarians, perhaps some students.
2. Volunteers (parents or students) to prepare sample copies of books, type book cards, make bookmarks, prepare flyers and notices.
3. Publicity committee: parents, students, or both.
4. Volunteers to staff the fair: take orders for books, handle money, keep records, order books from supplier, receive books, and transmit books to those who have ordered them.
5. A committee or secretary to coordinate all the work of other committees and volunteers.

MATERIALS NEEDED:

1. Sample books, for display and examination. These should be grouped in appropriate categories of subject matter and difficulty.
2. Typed record cards for each book, recording author, title, publisher, and price. Index cards may be large enough—4×6″ or 5×8″.
3. Bookmarks for displayed books, with the notice: "For Display Only. Do not remove from exhibit room."
4. Flyers and other publicity material, prepared with the approval of the school administration, to announce the Fair, and to maintain interest.

5. Order blanks (duplicate or triplicate order pads save work).
6. Receipt books (duplicate pads are useful).

DIRECTIONS:

1. The book-selection committee, working with the district and/or school librarian, gets in touch with a book jobber or wholesaler and arranges to get sample books for display and examination. The selection should include a number of low-priced books that will be both attractive and within the capacity of students and parents to buy. The books chosen should include some for all grade levels in the school. The supplier should have an adequate stock of all books displayed.
2. Books should be placed in the teachers' lounge so teachers may examine them at leisure before the Book Fair.
3. Members of the publicity committee, or other volunteers, visit the classrooms (at a time arranged with each teacher) to tell students about the Book Fair and perhaps read a short portion from at least one of the books that will be shown.
4. The Book Fair is held in the library, in the Instructional Materials Center, or in a nearby room each afternoon from 2:00 to 4:00 for two weeks. The Fair should also be open at least one evening. Parent volunteers and student librarians staff the sale, taking book orders and handling money.

BOOKSELLING PROCEDURE:

1. The person who takes the order for a book records the buyer's name, classroom, and home telephone number on the record card. (As far as possible, a student should be the buyer of record for a member of his family or other adult.)

2. A receipt is given to the purchaser for all money received, and a duplicate receipt is kept.
3. The person in charge of the Fair staff on any day is responsible for balancing money received with orders and receipt.
4. At the end of the day orders are sent to the book supplier with money to pay for them. The school's credit is not used for getting these books.
5. When books are received from the supplier, a person or committee chosen for the work distributes the books to those who ordered them. It may be wise to get a receipt for the delivered book.

■ WRITTEN BOOK REPORT (2-6)

BEHAVIORAL OBJECTIVE: To learn what to include in a written book report.

MATERIALS NEEDED:
1. Teacher-prepared worksheets.
2. File for completed reports.

DIRECTIONS:
1. The student completes worksheets where blanks have been left for him to supply:
    a. Author
    b. Title
    c. Publisher
    d. Copyright date
    e. Number of pages
    f. Date reading of book began; date completed
    g. A brief account (2 to 5 sentences) of the story plot or the essential content of the book
    h. His own name

2. Reports can be filed in a variety of ways such as:
   a. Main Dewey nonfiction classes and fiction categories
   b. Subject categories
   c. Last names of students
   d. Month completed

■ READING ROUND-UP (3-4)

BEHAVIORAL OBJECTIVES:
1. To acquire interest in recreational reading.
2. To learn what a brand is.

MATERIALS NEEDED:
1. Charts.
2. Brand name stamps and stamp pad.

DIRECTIONS:
1. The class is divided into two, three, or four groups according to birth months.
2. Each group selects a book-related team name (such as The Speedy Readers, The Bookworms, The Reading Riders).
3. The teacher has a rubber stamp made with either the team name or a symbol the children may design for their group.

4. The students read books according to an agreed plan and submit individual or team reports.

5. The brand is stamped on each book report before it is filed.
6. Each group has a chart showing its brand and name, as shown. A "books read" list is posted near this.
7. The class may stage several round-ups during the school year: Book Week, National Library Week, End of the School Year, or other selected occasion.

■ TOP TEN (2-6)

BEHAVIORAL OBJECTIVES:

1. To motivate reading.
2. To utilize title-page information.

MATERIALS NEEDED:

1. "Ballots"—slips of paper with blank spaces for title, author, illustrator, and publisher.
2. "Ballot boxes"—one for each grade level participating.

DIRECTIONS:

1. Students cast votes for books they have read and liked.
2. Ballots must be correctly completed and signed.
3. Periodically the votes are counted and the results posted along with names of the students who have voted for the winning books.

   Note: This is a good student project for library assistants.

■ POPULARITY POLL (3-6)

BEHAVIORAL OBJECTIVES:

1. To identify favorite books.
2. To identify favorite authors.
3. To identify favorite illustrators.
4. To identify favorite types of books.
5. To gather current information about student

reading preferences useful for graded summer reading lists.

MATERIALS NEEDED: 1. Slips of colored paper upon which the following has been duplicated:

Grade__________ Boy or Girl__________
What is the best book you have ever read? __________
____
Who is your favorite author? __________
What is your favorite type of book (dog stories; romance, horses, mystery stories—write one) __________
Do you like illustrations in books? __________
Who is your favorite illustrator? __________

2. Box in library as central collection spot.

DIRECTIONS:
1. Collect information during spring months (March-May).
2. Tabulate results before school ends.
3. Distribute as summer reading lists.

■ AN ALPHABET OF CHILDREN'S CLASSICS (4-6)

BEHAVIORAL OBJECTIVES:
1. To acquaint students with classics.
2. To review alphabetical order.

MATERIALS NEEDED:
1. Prepared lists of 26 questions for students to try to solve.
2. Key to check answers.

DIRECTIONS: Children must answer each question or statement with a title, author, character, or fact from the "classics" in children's literature.

An example of an Alphabet of Children's Classics:

The answers given in parentheses are not given to the students. The first answer begins with A, the second with B, and so on. (Disregard A, An, The.)

1. Famous stories told to save the life of the teller. (*Arabian Nights*)
2. A title which is a horse's name. (*Black Beauty*)
3. One of Dickens' most loved stories. (*A Christmas Carol*)
4. An erratic gentleman from Spain. (Don Quixote)
5. Who searched a lifetime for her lover? (Evangeline)
6. The kind of stories for which Aesop is famous. (*Fables*)
7. The Italian shoemaker who loved Pinocchio. (Geppetto)
8. A boy whose name is associated with a pair of silver skates. (Hans Brinker)
9. Important character in *The Legend of Sleepy Hollow*. (Ichabod Crane)
10. A famous book about animals in India. (*Jataka Tales*)
11. The founder of the Round Table. (King Arthur)
12. A friend of *Little Women*. (Laurie)
13. A brave soldier who sent another man to do his wooing. (Miles Standish)
14. The name of a boy who rode on the back of a goose. (Nils)
15. The story of a brave warrior's return after the Trojan War. (*The Odyssey*)
16. A rich boy and a poor boy who changed places. (*The Prince and the Pauper*)
17. The name of a famous search by Thor and Loki. (The Quest of the Hammer)
18. Who had a twenty-year nap? (Rip Van Winkle)
19. What book told of a family shipwrecked on a desert island? (*The Swiss Family Robinson*)
20. An author of favorite dog stories. (Terhune, Albert Payson)
21. Who told the stories about the Tar Baby, Bre'r Rabbit and Red Fox? (Uncle Remus)
22. Title of book about a certain doctor's trip to Africa. (*Voyages of Dr. Dolittle*)
23. Who for a time kept house in the tree-tops for a boy who never grew up? (Wendy)
24. Few words begin with "X" but you will meet one in a science-fiction title by André Norton. (*The X-Factor*)
25. The name of a young Chinese boy. (Young Fu)
26. The father of the Greek gods who lived on Mount Olympus. (Zeus)

■ PICTORIAL BOOK REPORT (1-4)

BEHAVIORAL OBJECTIVE: To keep a graphic record of books read.

MATERIALS NEEDED:
1. Butcher paper 18 inches wide by 3 yards long.
2. Crayons.
3. White paper ($8^1/_2 \times 11''$).

DIRECTIONS:
1. Fold butcher paper in accordion folds 11 inches wide, as though folding paper for a fan.
2. Children use the white paper to draw original illustrations for books they read (characters of the story, a favorite part, or the like).
3. One illustration is pasted on each section of the folded butcher paper, reserving one section to fold over the completed project.
4. At the end of the year the child's collection of these projects represents his reading for the year.

■ MULTIMEDIA BOOK REPORT (3-5)

BEHAVIORAL OBJECTIVES:
1. To learn to retell events of a story in sequence.
2. To be able to interpret a story graphically.
3. To apply the skills of photography.
4. To apply tape-recording skills.

MATERIALS NEEDED:*
1. Paper
2. Art media such as crayons or wet chalk.
3. Camera
4. Tape recorder

*Obtaining and managing these materials is a creative activity for a classroom parent aide.

DIRECTIONS:
1. Two or three students agree to read a book and illustrate its main events.
2. They plan and execute their illustrations.
3. They plan and prepare a script to accompany their illustrations including:
   a. Their own names in the introduction.
   b. The author and title of the book they have chosen.
   c. The reason for their selection.
   d. Some appropriate background music if desired.
4. They practice taping the script until they have a satisfactory tape.
5. They make slides of illustrations.
6. They practice synchronization of slides and tape.
7. They present their final product to the class.

■ MUSIC-APPRECIATION CONTEST (3-Up)

BEHAVIORAL OBJECTIVES:
1. To become better acquainted with the school record collection.
2. To recognize well-known music, classical and otherwise.
3. To appreciate a wide variety of music.
4. To learn about composers.

MATERIALS NEEDED:
1. Recorded cassette tapes of each of the pieces to be included in the study.
2. Short informational material on each selection.
3. Short informational material on each composer.
4. Cassette players available for overnight loan.
5. Promotional announcements of "forthcoming" contest.
6. Appropriate displays in the library.

DIRECTIONS: 1. The librarian arranges with each classroom teacher to visit the classroom and to play excerpts of some of the tapes, discuss the rules of the contest, and urge student participation.

2. Two selections are featured each week:
   a. Bulletins with information about the compositions and the composers are supplied to each class.
   b. Tapes are played during recess and before and after school in the library. (No other music is played during these times.)
   c. Cassette players and tapes are available for overnight loan.
   d. Children may listen to music, using headsets, at any time when the library is open.

3. When all selections have been introduced and there has been enough time for study, the date for the testing is announced.
   a. The test is given in the multimedia center to those interested in participation. (See the example that follows.)
   b. Winners are not *necessarily* limited to contestants with perfect scores.
   c. Prizes may be a field trip to a local musical event, a party with music and refreshments, an appearance by a musician performing in the local media center.

Example of test for a music-appreciation contest:

Each selection of music will be played for you to listen to for a few minutes. As it is being played a letter will be held up. You are to decide what the name of the music is, write that letter in the blank beside the name, then put the same letter beside the name of the person who composed the music.

Barcarole (*from* Tales of Hoffman) ______	John Philip Sousa ______
Take the A Train ______	American jazz composer, unknown ______

Greensleeves ______
On the Trail (*from* Grand Canyon Suite) ______
West Side Story ______
Nutcracker Suite ______
When the Saints Go Marching In ______
Surprise Symphony ______
Carmen ______
The Stars and Stripes Forever ______
The Moldau ______

Georges Bizet ______
Ferde Grofé ______
Bedrich Smetana ______
Jacques Offenbach ______
Franz Joseph Haydn ______
An Olde English Folksong ______
Peter Ilich Tchaikovsky ______
Duke Ellington ______
Leonard Bernstein ______

■ ART-PRINT APPRECIATION CONTEST (3-Up)

BEHAVIORAL OBJECTIVES:

1. To become better acquainted with the school art-print collection.
2. To recognize paintings by their content and style.
3. To appreciate a wide variety of art.
4. To recognize and learn about famous artists.

MATERIALS NEEDED:

1. A selection of ten or twelve art prints with appeal to children for display in the materials center.
2. Short informational material on each selection.
3. Short informational material on each artist.
4. Promotional announcements in advance of contest and a series of follow-up bulletins.

DIRECTIONS:

1. Children take initiative in studying art prints on display in library. (Some classroom teachers are very active in extending study in the classroom.)
2. When there has been enough time for children to learn the names of the painting and the painter, the date of the contest test is announced.

3. Those *interested* in participating are invited to try the test.
4. The prizes are announced.
5. Parents are invited to test themselves if they wish.
6. The paintings on display have any titles or artist's signatures covered and have letters of the alphabet attached as their identifying marks.

Example of an art-print test:

Below are the list of paintings on the left and the list of painters on the right. They are all mixed up. Put the letter of the painting in the correct author blank.

A. Children's Games	______ Gainsborough
B. Pinkie	______ Van Gogh
C. The Night Watch	______ Breughel
D. Self Portrait	______ Lawrence
E. Broadway Boogie-Woogie	______ Picasso
F. Still Life	______ Rembrandt
G. The Blue Boy	______ Mondrian
H. Flowers in Stone	______ Dürer
I. Young Hare	______ Feininger
J. The Church	______ Klee

■ BOOK INFORMATION, PLEASE! (7-8)

BEHAVIORAL OBJECTIVE: To promote interest in children's literature.

MATERIALS NEEDED:
1. A quiz of 25 items related to the field of children's literature.
2. Answer key.

Example of a quiz sheet for Book Information, Please!

Here are questions taken from well-known books. Every right answer counts 4 points. If you answer all of them, your score is 100.

1. With what books do you associate the following places? (a) Dorfli, (b) Lilliput, (c) Puddleby.
2. In what story does a boy fire a gun loaded with nails, buttons, and pins to protect his family?
3. Name two rabbits famous in literature who might deliver your Easter eggs on Easter morning.
4. Name the story in which this event takes place: A tin soldier is swallowed by a fish.
5. Name the books which these places suggest: (a) Centerburg, (b) Sherwood Forest.
6. What do these three characters have in common: Pinocchio, Hitty, and Miss Hickory?
7. In what book do we find Laura telling of her early childhood in a log cabin in Wisconsin?
8. In what book is a plate the most beautiful thing in a little girl's life?
9. In what kind of books are the characters Pecos Bill, Paul Bunyan, and John Henry and what do they have in common?
10. In Bookland you may have met the following dogs. Tell what kind of dogs they are and who is the author of the books in which these dogs are found? (a) Big Red, (b) Buck, (c) Silver Chief, (d) Bob, (e) Lad.
11. In the book *The Saturdays,* by Elizabeth Enright, what kind of special entertainment did Rush Melindy attend?
12. In what story does Nate Twitchell save Uncle Beazley's life?
13. What name does not belong in the following list and why? Eric Knight, Albert P. Terhune, Jack O'Brien, Kate Seredy.
14. With what kind of animal stores do you associate the name Henry?
15. Who said: (a) "I want the moon." (b) "Humph!"
16. If you were to see this advertisement, of what book would it remind you?

    Reed and Glass, Inc.
    PURE AND APPLIED RESEARCH
17. What book does not belong in this list although all of them have one thing in common: *How Baseball Began in Brooklyn, Casey at the Bat, Long Stretch at First Base, All-American, Keystone Kids.*

18. In what famous story does the name of the day of the week become the name of a man?
19. What kind of factory did Charlie want to become involved with?
20. If you were at sea in Bookland and you saw a ship named *The Dawn Treader* and another named *Hispaniola,* of what books would they remind you?
21. True or false: The *Tough Winter* is the sequel to *Rabbit Hill.*
22. Whose biography would you be reading if it were about a noted Venetian traveler who was the globe trotter of the Middle Ages?
23. If you were to meet a boy named Jody with his fawn named Flag, what book would you be in?
24. What characters became involved in a murder while burying a dead cat?
25. What special talent did the cricket have in George Selden's book *The Cricket in Times Square*?

Key to the preceding example:

1. (a) *Heidi* (Spyri), (b) *Gulliver's Travels* (Swift), (c) *The Story of Dr. Doolittle* (Lofting).
2. *The Matchlock Gun* (Edmonds).
3. *Peter Rabbit* (Potter); *The Country Bunny* (Heyward).
4. "The Steadfast Tin Soldier" (Andersen).
5. (a) *Homer Rice* or *Centerburg Tales* (McCloskey); (b) *The Merry Adventures of Robin Hood* (Pyle).
6. All are made of wood.
7. *The Little House in the Big Woods* (Wilder).
8. *The Blue Willow* (Gates).
9. Tall tales. All imaginary or all American.
10. (a) Irish setter (Kjelgaard), (b) husky (London), (c) half husky, half wolf (O'Brien), (d) sheep dog (Ollivant), (e) collie (Terhune).
11. The opera.
12. *The Enormous Egg* (Butterworth).
13. Kate Seredy, because she is the only woman author listed and also because she is not a famous author of dog stories.
14. Horse stories.

15. (a) Princess Lenore in *Many Moms* (Thurber). (b) The camel in "How the Camel Got His Hump" in *Just So Stories* by Kipling.
16. *Henry Reed, Inc.*, by Robertson.
17. *All-American,* because it is about football, not baseball.
18. *Robinson Crusoe* (Friday).
19. Chocolate factory.
20. *The Tales of Narnia* (C. S. Lewis), *Treasure Island* (R. L. Stevenson).
21. True.
22. Marco Polo.
23. *The Yearling* (Rawlings).
24. Tom Sawyer and Huck Finn in the book, *Tom Sawyer.*
25. He could sing opera.

■ SOME WAYS TO CREATE INTEREST IN FREE INDEPENDENT READING

GROUP DISCUSSIONS

Favorite books, authors, illustrators.
Recommendations for school purchase.
Panel discussions about prize winners and runners-up.
"Best seller" television panel show.
Special-interest reports: for example, horses, mystery, sports, humor, ecology.

HANDICRAFTS —ART WORK

Decorative reading lists, bookmarks, book plates.
Peep-hole shows.
Stitchery.
Dressing dolls.
Dioramas.
Posters, murals. friezes.
Characters: drawings, models, carving, silhouettes.
Models: famous ships, other vehicles.
Illustrations—collecting and making.
Student-made books.

FIELD TRIPS

Book bindery.
Public library.
Printer.
Newspaper.
Other school libraries.

DISPLAYS

Bulletin boards:
  a. simple, interesting, eye-catching.
  b. frequently changed.
  c. definite message, easily understood.
  d. book-related.
New books.
Seasonal books.
Private collections.
Unusual books.
Special authors.
Special illustrators.
Relating books to nonbook media.

DRAMATIC ILLUSTRATIONS

Talks by guest authors.
Pantomime.
Charades.
Puppet shows.
Recordings.
Reading to younger students.
Flannel-board presentation.
Student plays.
Professional performances.
Television specials; educational television.
Story telling.
Student-made movies.
Student-made slide-tape presentations.

WRITTEN EXPRESSION

Column in school newspaper.
Blurbs, sales advertisements.
Reasons for recommending purchase.
Letters to authors or illustrators (in care of publishers).
Reviews for magazines.

CLUBS	Student library assistant. Hobby (for example cooking, model building, stamp collecting). Mystery Readers club. Animal Lovers club.
GAMES	Student-made. Teacher-made. Commercial.
ACTIVITIES	Student book store (paperbacks, posters). Book fairs.

MISCELLANEOUS

■ BOOK AUCTION (4-6)

BEHAVIORAL OBJECTIVE: To read books and stimulate others to read them.

MATERIALS NEEDED: Two charts, one each for "Books Sold" and "Books Bought."

DIRECTIONS:

1. A student who has read a book tries to "sell" it by auction to the class.
2. He tells the class an interesting part of the book—just enough to get others to want to read the book. Or instead of telling, he may read a portion of the book to the class.
3. Members of the class may ask some questions about the book—*not*, however, about plot or characters. Example: How many pages?
4. Students bid to "buy" the book: Two days' reading time to complete it. Or three days. Or more.
5. When the bid reading time is up, the student who sold the book asks questions about it of the buyer. If the questions are answered satisfactorily, both seller and buyer get a point on the "Book Sold" and "Book Bought" charts.

Variations: The "seller" may be allowed to judge the satisfactory quality of the answers. Or instead, a committee of "auditors" (students who know the book) may judge the answers or even put the questions.

■ BOOK HANGMAN (2-6)

BEHAVIORAL OBJECTIVE: To guess familiar book titles.

MATERIALS NEEDED: Chalkboard and chalk.

DIRECTIONS: This game is played like Hangman, in that one player tries to "hang" another by drawing a noose and gallows, adding successive parts of a hanging person—head, then torso, then arms, then legs, perhaps hands, feet. One part of the body is drawn for each mistake. The Hangman wins if he can hang a whole body; the competitor wins if he can guess a book title correctly before the Hangman completes the body.

1. A student selected to be Hangman draws a set of blank spaces on the chalkboard, one for each letter in a book title. Example:

   — — — — — — — —

   — — — — — — — — — — —

   (These spaces can be filled with *Danny and the Dinosaur*.)
2. The Hangman gives some hint of the title and a student attempts to guess what it is and to fill the letter spaces, one at a time.
3. The Hangman writes each correctly guessed letter where it belongs. If the guesser makes

a mistake, "his" head is drawn at the noose; if another, "his" torso; and so on until he either guesses the title correctly or is completely hanged. If he is hanged, another contestant tries; if he is correct, be becomes Hangman and someone tries to guess his title.

4. The contestant may challenge the Hangman if he suspects that the book title is imaginary. The card catalog may be used to verify the title, or a committee rules on the challenge; either the Hangman or the challenger loses.

Variation: The Hangman may be given a title from a list or a set of cards instead of choosing his own title.

■ GIRL SCOUT BOOK BADGE (4-Up)

Teachers and librarians can make this badge available and meaningful for interested Girl Scouts or use the format as a general class project. The following is an interpretation of the requirements found in the *Girl Scouts Handbook*.

1. Have students establish an approved reading plan in a subject area of interest to them. (*Examples:* Horses, Famous Women, Girls of Long Ago, Modern Mystery, Sports, Music, Romance)
2. Ten books must be read and reports submitted in a given time limit.
3. When the books have been read, the student must be able to categorize three of them as among the following: adventure, travel, mystery, biography, or other subject.
4. Verification of library skills, such as use of card catalog and familiarity with arrangement of books, is necessary.
5. A display using books as a theme is required.

6. Some study of illustrators must be made. This requirement can be met through filmstrip and 16mm film viewing or by book talks on a special author (for instance, Maurice Sendak) for a lower-grade audience.
7. The Book Badge candidate must design an original bookplate for herself.

■ GIRL SCOUT STORYTELLING BADGE (4-Up)

The following merit-badge criteria can be used as the framework for establishing a storytelling band of students as well as for earning the Storytelling Badge.

1. As each of ten different collections of folk and fairy tales is read, the author, title, and call number are entered on a 3″×5″ card. In addition the reader selects from the collection the story she would most like to tell. Notation is made of the title and page numbers for future reference.
2. After the ten collections have been read, the prospective storyteller confers with the teacher or librarian about a story to learn for telling. The telling must fill more than ten minutes but less than twenty minutes. (Reading the story aloud slowly and expressively, accompanied by a kitchen timer helps determine this time limit.)
3. The student is responsible for listening to a live story (as at a public library or from television), or using available recordings of stories being told.
4. When the story is selected, the teacher or librarian helps the student make a list of words whose meaning or use add flavor and character to the story. These words must be looked up and pronunciations checked.
5. When the student is ready, a class is scheduled and the storyteller's debut is made.
6. It has been found helpful to have the rest of the candidates accompany the novice and to allow time after the session to make a constructive evaluation of the experience.

■ LIBRARY QUIZ (4-6)

PROJECT OBJECTIVE: To test or reinforce knowledge about library resources.

MATERIALS NEEDED:
1. Copies of a quiz.
2. Answer keys for self-correction.

Example of a library quiz:

1. The quickest way to find out whether the book entitled *Little Vic* is in the library is to look in the card catalog drawer marked (a) Co-Di; (b) Li-Ma; (c) Ja-La.
2. A list of topics in a book arranged in alphabetical order is: (a) the index; (b) the table of contents; (c) the preface.
3. Fiction is arranged alphabetically on the shelf by: (a) author; (b) subject; (c) title.
4. The system in general use for classifying books is called: (a) the Dewey decimal system; (b) the Library of Congress system; (c) the expansive system.
5. To find out what books the library has about China, you should first: (a) look among the geography books; (b) look in the card catalog; (c) ask another student.
6. Nonfiction books in a library are grouped by: (a) subject; (b) size; (c) title.
7. Individual biography is arranged alphabetically by (a) person written about; (b) title; (c) author.
8. To find the title of a book written by Sir James Barrie, you should look in the card catalog under: (a) James; (b) Sir; (c) Barrie.
9. The quickest way to find the page on which a certain topic appears in a book is through: (a) the title page; (b) the index; (c) the contents.
10. To find out whether or not the library has the book called *The Mystery of the Missing Goat,* you would look under the word: (a) Goat; (b) The; (c) Mystery.
11. What are three ways that you can use to locate a book in the library?

    a. ______________________________

b. ____________________

c. ____________________

12. How can you tell the difference between a fiction and nonfiction book?

    ____

13. The *Abridged Reader's Guide* helps you to locate information in: (a) atlases; (b) magazines; (c) almanacs.
14. The only useful materials in school and public libraries are books and magazines. True______ False______
15. An 8mm film loop is: (a) funny; (b) silent; (c) large.
16. The Caldecott Medal is given each year to a(n): (a) illustrator; (b) swimmer; (c) newspaper.
17. Which book would *not* be useful if you were looking up "Chemistry"? (a) *Book of Popular Science;* (b) *Young People's Science Encyclopedia;* (c) *Junior Book of Authors.*
18. A filmstrip's copyright date is usually found: (a) at the beginning; (b) at the end; (c) on the container.
19. Overlays are found on: (a) slides; (b) transparencies; (c) art prints.
20. Which of these will *not* usually be found in an atlas? (a) population; (b) capitals of countries; (c) presidents of the United States.
21. If you wanted to know who won the World Series two years ago, you would look in: (a) an almanac; (b) an atlas; (c) the card catalog.
22. The list of book and nonbook references at the end of a report or encyclopedia article is called: (a) an autobiography; (b) a bibliography; (c) a biography.
23. Most study prints usually have helpful information: (a) on the cover; (b) in the teacher's guide; (c) on the back.

Key to the preceding example:

1. b
2. a
3. a
4. a
5. b
6. a
7. a
8. c
9. b
10. c
11. author, subject, title
12. numbers on spine or pocket
13. b
14. false

15. b
16. a
17. c
18. a
19. b
20. c
21. a
22. b
23. c

■ SHOW CARDS OF AUTHORS (4-6)

MATERIALS NEEDED:

1. Each child has twelve pieces of paper on his desk in front of him.
2. Six pieces of the paper will have names of authors on them; six others will have names of books on them.

DIRECTIONS: When the leader asks the students to show a certain title (for instance, *Paddle-to-the-Sea*), the child with that title will hold it up and the child having the name of "Holling Clancy Holling" on one of his papers will hold it up to match with the first child's paper.

■ AUTHOR BOARD OR MAP (5)

MATERIALS NEEDED: A large map of the United States

DIRECTIONS: As children study about the authors of the library books they are reading, they write the name of the author on a small card and pin it on the state in which the author was born.

This game is especially good for students studying the United States, as it ties in with a Social Studies unit.

SELECTED BIBLIOGRAPHY

Boyd, Jessie, and others. *Books, Libraries and You*. Third edition. New York: Charles Scribner's Sons, 1965. A handbook on the use of reference books and library reference resources.

Gaver, Mary Virginia (ed.). *The Elementary School Library Collection; a Guide to Books and Other Media,* Phases 1, 2, 3. Williamsport, Pennsylvania: Bro-Dart Foundation, 1972. A comprehensive listing of book and nonbook materials for purchase by elementary-school libraries, with recommendations for first purchase (Phase 1), second purchase (Phase 2), and additional titles (Phase 3). Each entry in the classified arrangement is in the form of a catalog card for the item. Revised every few years, with annual supplements between revisions. Includes subject, author, title indices.

Harshaw, Ruth H. *In What Book?* New York: The Macmillan Company, 1970. Contains questions and answers about books for ages three to sixteen; designed as a quiz game to stimulate reading.

Hodges, Elizabeth D. (ed.). *Books for Elementary School Libraries: An Initial Collection.* Chicago: American Library Association, 1969. Annotations for over 3,000 books describe their contents, suggest relevance to curriculum, indicate grade levels and buying information.

Hopkinson, Shirley L. *Instructional Materials for Teaching the Use of the Library*. Fourth edition. San Jose, California, Claremont House, 1971. Guide to print (books) and nonprint materials such as films, slides, filmstrips, transparencies, charts, and tapes.

Kemp, Jerrold E., and colleagues. *Planning and Producing Audiovisual Materials*. Second Edition. San Francisco: Chandler Publishing Company, 1968. (Since 1971 available from

Intext College Publishers, Scranton, Pennsylvania 18515.) Simple step-by-step instructions on making all kinds of audiovisual materials for educational purposes.

Learning to Use Media. Bulletin 197. Madison, Wisconsin: Wisconsin Department of Public Instruction, 1970. Describes media experiences appropriate for different grade levels.

McDaniel, Roderick (ed.) *Resources for Learning:* A core media collection for elementary schools. New York: R. R. Bowker, 1971. A selective annotated guide to 4,000 recommended titles in different media for grade levels K-6.

Minor, Ed. *Simplified Techniques for Preparing Visual Instructional Materials.* New York: McGraw-Hill, 1963. Designed to aid the person without skills in art, graphic art, or photographic techniques as well as the professional.

Santa, Beauel M. and Lois Lynn Hardy. *How to Use the Library.* Second edition. Palo Alto, California: Pacific Books, 1966. A series of lessons and activities designed to provide basic library instruction for junior and senior high school students.

Scott, Marian H. *Periodicals for School Libraries: A Guide to Magazines, Newspapers, and Periodical Indexes.* Chicago: American Library Association, 1969. Evaluates over 400 periodicals for children and young adults from kindergarten through high school. Corresponds to curricular needs and wide range of reading levels. Includes key foreign and ethnic periodicals.

Rufsvold, Margaret I. and Carolyn Guss. *Guides to Educational Media.* Third edition. Chicago: American Library Association, 1971. Annotated guide to the wide variety of nonprint materials available.

Toser, Marie A. *A Library Manual: A Study-Work Manual of Lessons on the Use of Books and Libraries.* Sixth edition. New York: H. W. Wilson Company, 1964. A series of ten units of instruction on the use of the library.

Using the Card Catalog. Produced by Hammond. Distributed by McGraw-Hill, 1969. Includes teacher's guide and 16 transparencies depicting alphabetical arrangement, types of cards, call numbers, and shelf arrangement for grades 4-9.

Using the Elementary School Library. Produced and distributed by Society for Visual Education, 1968. Filmstrips, phonodiscs, or tape cassettes provide library instruction in a media center for print and nonprint material. Grades 4-6.

Using the Library Series. Chicago: Encyclopaedia Britannica Educational Corporation, 1970. Color filmstrips in this series show use of the card catalog, classification of books, using the dictionary, encyclopedia, and special reference books. For intermediate grades.